Dear Tom …

Dear Tom ...

Letters to an enquiring Christian

John Legg

 EVANGELICAL PRESS

EVANGELICAL PRESS
12 Wooler Street, Darlington, Co. Durham, DL1 1RQ,
England

© Evangelical Press 1990
First published 1990

British Library Cataloguing in Publication Data
Legg, John
　　Dear Tom...
　　1. Church of England. Calvinism. Christian doctrine
　　I. Title
　　230.3

　　ISBN 0-85234-275-6

Cover pictures reproduced by courtesy of Rex Features.

Printed in Great Britain by Cox and Wyman Ltd, Reading.

To
Dave and Sue
to encourage them
in their labours.

Contents

Introduction

The substance of the following letters was published in the *Evangelical Times* during 1987. In the light of comments at the time it is felt that the Christian public would benefit from reading the whole of the correspondence between Uncle Harry and his nephew Tom.

1.

To God be the glory

Dear Tom,

I hardly know how to reply to your most
welcome letter! So you have become a Christian at last! You can have no idea how much
this rejoices my heart — and your aunt joins
with me — especially as your letter gives
good reason to hope that this is a genuine
work of God.

I am pleased you delayed a little, until
you were reasonably sure that you had really
come to know the Lord. To the evidences
you give about loving to read and hear God's
Word and delighting in both prayer and the
company of God's people, I would add the
fact that you have written to me! The breach
between us over the last not so few years,
while you have been going your own way,
has been a great grief to us both, especially
since your parents died and we have felt
somewhat responsible for you. (Yes, I know
that you are not a child or even a very young
man any longer, but one never loses this
sense of duty towards the family.) At last our
prayers have been answered.

Of course, I shall be delighted to give you any help that I can. I am only sorry that we are so far away that anything I can say will have to be by letter. I am naturally delighted that you have found a welcome in the church where you were converted and that you already feel at home there. That, of course, is the best place to learn and to begin to serve your Lord, but it may be that an uncle's help will not come amiss.

Current problems

I notice that you have already found that there are many strange ideas around. I suppose there has never been a time when the church was free from confusion and heresy, but I really do think that today is worse than most times since the Reformation. We not only have the old problems of Roman Catholic traditions but also the complete rejection of the Scriptures as our authority by many who call themselves Protestants. Add to that the number of sects that have sprung up like mushrooms — or toadstools — over the last century or so, and you have a fine state of affairs.

Even more confusing, if that were possible, and indescribably sad, is the state of those who do accept the Bible as their authority, or at least claim to do so — those known as evangelicals. There is such a departing from the old ways that I sometimes think that if our forefathers were to come back they would not recognize us as their children. There are weird and wonderful ideas abroad and both evangelical

There has never been a time when the church was free from confusion and heresy, but I really do think that today is worse than most times since the Reformation.

preachers and evangelical writers are spreading teachings which until this century were regarded as heresy, but are now treated as orthodoxy.

I mustn't worry you with these aberrations at this stage, but you need to be aware of the situation and not take everything on trust. Refer everything to the Scriptures — and if I can help you to do this, I shall be only too pleased.

Salvation is from the Lord

One thing in particular concerns me at this moment. There was so much in your letter about what the preacher did and what you did, but little or nothing of what God has done. We must be careful to give God the glory, for salvation is his work, from beginning to end. The stress today seems to be entirely on what man does, when, in fact, unless God enables him he is not free to do anything! The gospel is really about God's coming and rescuing helpless sinners. You will remember this from your recent reading in Paul's letter to the Romans. (I'm pleased that you have begun there; it is not easy, but it is basic to everything else and if you do persevere it will give you a good foundation for your Christian life.) Romans 1:16 tells us that the gospel 'is the power of God for the salvation of everyone who believes'. And in this letter 'salvation' includes everything from forgiveness and justification to the final glory.

Of course, it is dangerous to base your beliefs on your experience, rather than the

We must be careful to give God the glory, for salvation is his work, from beginning to end.

> *Jesus said that he came 'to seek and to save what was lost' (Luke 19:10).*

Word of God, but it is also true that when you believe the Scriptures, you find that your own experience confirms their truth. What I am referring to is this: you must be aware that although you did seek Christ in the end, it was God who started the seeking. He took the initiative. Before you began seriously to consider becoming a Christian, the Lord had stirred up your family and friends to pray for you. Before you wanted to have your sins forgiven, the Lord was showing you how empty and purposeless your life was. It was he who led you to the right contacts and who showed you what the Christian life was really like. It was he who took away the props which had supported you, apparently, until that time and it was he who directed your steps towards the right church where you heard the gospel. It was no accident that the preacher chose that particular subject on the evening you went to the service, but above all it was not your intelligence that enabled you to understand what had previously been nonsense to you, but God who enlightened you.

I'm thankful to say that there are many who, although they do not understand all that the Bible teaches about God's sovereignty, do acknowledge that before they sought God, he sought them. (After all, Jesus himself said that he came 'to seek and to save what was lost', Luke 19:10.) The apostle Paul makes a point of this in Galatians 4:9, where he qualifies what he has said, lest he should give the wrong impression: 'But now that you know God — or rather are known *by* God ... ' To acknowledge this in experience is at least a good beginning, if you then go on to understand more deeply God's way of salvation from the Scriptures. Ultimately, of course, this is a mystery, but we can go quite a long way, if we are willing to follow the Scriptures as far as they lead us. And this we must do, for it is the only way that God receives from us the glory he deserves.

Credit where credit is due

Since this is so I hope that you are full of thankfulness and praise that God has saved you, and that you will be careful in the way you refer to your conversion, making sure that you give credit where credit is due — and that is not to yourself! This is in no way intended to put you down; I am truly thrilled to hear from you with your news and want to do all I can to encourage you. The fact is that the best way to help you is to make you realize more fully your dependence on God and the fact that he can be depended on fully. In this way you will progress better in holiness and assurance, and so in joy also.

Yours at last in the family of God,

Uncle Harry

I hope that you are full of thankfulness and praise that God has saved you.

2.

Free but a slave

Dear Tom,

Thank you for your recent letter. I was pleased to hear of your progress in the faith since your last 'epistle' and especially that you are trying to witness at work. I'll do my best to answer your questions — I've never been worried by questions since I realized that people respect you if you say you don't know, instead of waffling — so long, of course, as you don't say it too often! It is good to raise your problems, for, apart from anything else, as you say, they affect what you do as well as what you think.

You're not the first, of course, to have problems with the subject of free will, nor will you be the last. The great humanist scholar, Erasmus, (a little before your time and even before mine!) had a long debate with Martin Luther about it all and, unintentionally, inspired the Reformer's great book, *The Bondage of the Will*. The controversy still rages, often rather bitterly, and crops up in various connections, so I'm not surprised that you have come across it already.

Before I deal with this, it may be helpful to

mention that the term 'Reformer' refers to
one of the leaders of the Reformation that
I mentioned in my first letter and that
puzzled you. The Reformation was the
great work of God during the sixteenth
century, when he restored his gospel to
the church after the darkness of the Middle
Ages. Martin Luther was his great instru-
ment in doing this, when he 'rediscovered'
the doctrine of justification by faith only
and the whole of Europe was transformed.
You would do well to read up about his
life and the Reformation which he sparked
off.

Suffering and free will

One difficult area affected by this issue is
the problem of suffering and I have a lot of
sympathy with what people say about free
will in this sphere. There is real truth in
asserting that man's free will is responsible for much of the suffering in the world
and we must beware of blaming God and
especially of making God the author of
sin. All the same, we must be cautious, as
it is possible to blame everything on man's
free will in such a way as to deny that God
has a hand in anything, e. g. in judgement.
If you do that, you end up without any
assurance that God is able and indeed
certain to triumph over evil in the end,
since, according to your reasoning, he has
no control over it.

So, while it may be technically accurate
to talk about free will in relation to God's
purpose and providence, so long as we
make certain things clear, it is nevertheless

*Martin
Luther
'rediscovered'
the doctrine
of
justification
by faith only
and the whole
of Europe
was
transformed.*

not to be recommended. The reason is that people are only too ready to transfer the idea to other areas, where it is quite wrong. (I'm thinking of the visiting evangelist you mentioned. More about that later!)

You may ask, 'What are these certain things that have to be made clear?' Let me elaborate. Men and women are not just pawns or robots, manipulated by an impersonal and fatalistic Supreme Being, but free agents. God does not compel anybody to do anything against his or her will. You and I decide what we want to do and are held responsible by God for what we do. On the other hand, God also is free and does what he has decided and planned to do. The question is, 'Whose will is final? Whose freedom is really absolute?' The answer must be that God's will is final, otherwise he is no longer God.

The First Cause

To use the language of the philosophers, God is the First Cause and works *through* our wills, decisions, words and deeds, as what are called 'second causes', without — mystery of mysteries — ever taking away our freedom or responsibility. So what we decide can never hinder, frustrate or thwart God's plans. God's will will be done. Did you ever hear about the lady who asked Spurgeon — I know you've heard of him! — if he really believed that what will be, will be. He answered, somewhat cheekily but truly, 'Madam, would you prefer me to believe that what will be, won't be?'

God does not compel anybody to do anything against his or her will.

This has to apply even to evil and sinful decisions and actions. The sinfulness attaches only to the second causes, not to God. Don't ask me how; I don't know. However, the fact is clear from the experience of Joseph. You remember how his brothers wickedly plotted against him and were responsible for selling him into slavery in Egypt. In the event this meant that he was able to interpret Pharaoh's dreams, store up grain and save, among others, the rest of his family and so keep the chosen line of Jacob alive. In Joseph's words, 'God sent me ahead of you to preserve for you a remnant on earth and to save your lives by a great deliverance' (Genesis 45:7). Later, in Genesis 50:20, he explains further: 'You intended to harm me, but God intended it for good to accomplish what is now being done, the saving of many lives.'

All things for good

This is the basis of such a wonderfully comforting verse as Romans 8:28 (which I hope you have learned by heart), about God working all things together for good, where 'all things' must include even the most wicked and sinful things, or else we are left without help and comfort just when we most need them. If you want further biblical evidence for this, look up Matthew 18:7: 'Woe to the world because of the things that cause people to sin! Such things must come'—the 'must' of divine purpose — 'but woe to the man through whom they come' — the 'woe' of human responsibility. It was always certain that

> *God working all things together for good must include even the most wicked and sinful things, or else we are left without help and comfort just when we most need them.*

Judas would betray Jesus, but God did not force him to do so and he bore the guilt for his action. It was God's plan and fixed purpose that Christ would be crucified; everyone admits that. Yet those who performed the crucifixion or, perhaps better, were the effective cause of it, the Jewish leaders, are called 'wicked' (Acts 2:23). On the same subject, Acts 4:28 speaks even more clearly: 'They did what your power and will had decided beforehand should happen.'

It would probably be better to call this free agency, rather than free will, or simply to stick to the term 'human responsibility'. In any case there is no way we frail humans can understand the matter. We can only trust and wonder. If we do, we gain great comfort, because the sovereign Lord is our heavenly Father. Now, on to the matter which really provokes controversy!

Free will and evangelism

Many earnest evangelists would tell you — one obviously has! — that denying free will 'cuts the nerve of evangelistic endeavour' and that there is no point in preaching or witnessing unless we believe men are free to respond. Now I have a lot of sympathy with their insistence on a real turning to God and their warning against putting the matter off. On the other hand it is very dangerous and most dishonouring to God to use the sort of language you quoted to me about God having done all he can to save them through sending Christ and 'now it all depends on them'. ('God's

We can only trust and wonder. If we do, we gain great comfort, because the sovereign Lord is our heavenly Father.

hands are tied' — indeed! Or even, as someone said recently, 'God is waiting for you to give him permission to give you the new birth!') Such language is almost blasphemous, giving the impression that God is frustrated and disappointed and the devil is master.

God's purpose is never frustrated and it includes the salvation of the elect — those whom he has predestined to believe in Christ — as we read in Acts 13:48: 'And all who were appointed for eternal life believed.' This is where we have to consider most carefully this matter of free will. Put very simply the state of affairs is this: man's will is free in the sense I've tried to describe; it is not forced or compelled, nor does it in any way have its responsibility removed. But when it comes to repenting and believing, or simply obeying God, that free will is a slave. (Hence the title of Luther's book.) It simply can't do what is required. Man cannot will to please God or truly turn to Christ. He has a sinful nature and is the slave of sin and the devil. See John 8:34: 'Everyone who sins is a slave to sin.'

Total inability

It is not God who prevents man from repenting; it is his own sinful heart that will not let him repent.

It is not God who prevents man from repenting; it is his own sinful heart that will not let him repent. He will not believe because he cannot believe, and he cannot believe because he will not believe. Just consider 1 Corinthians 2:14: 'The man without the Spirit ['the natural man' in the

AV] does not accept the things that come from the Spirit of God, for they are foolishness to him and he cannot understand them, because they are spiritually discerned.' Notice the 'cannot' and see that this inability is because of his sinful nature before he is born again. Then turn to Romans 8:7-8: 'The sinful mind [the mind of the unbeliever] is hostile to God. It does not submit to God's law, nor can it do so. Those controlled by the sinful nature cannot please God.' Notice again the 'cannot's. How foolish, then, to rely on man's free will! The will freely expresses the nature and desires of the man. But the nature is bound in sin, so the will also is free only to sin. The term free will is best forgotten.

I know what you're going to say next: 'What's the point of witnessing then?' or more positively, 'How does anyone become a Christian?' or even more practically, 'What should I say to the unbeliever?' The answer to all three questions lies in the gracious and powerful working of the Holy Spirit. When we preach or witness we rely on him to open blind eyes, to change hearts and wills — all without violating man's personality or responsibility — so that men do, willingly, repent and believe. Our confidence is that God uses the Word of God on our lips to do this. Amazingly, our witnessing or preaching is used to deliver men from their bondage. What we say in calling upon men to repent and believe rests on our faith in this mysterious working.

What's the point of witnessing?

Ability and responsibility

It is important to avoid two errors, at opposite extremes. The first error is that of equating ability with responsibility. (Don't worry! That's not as difficult as it sounds.) At first sight, it seems very reasonable to argue that since men are told to repent, i. e. are responsible to do so, then they must be able to do so or it isn't fair. Again from the other end, it seems reasonable to say that if men can't repent, then they shouldn't be commanded to repent, and since they can't accept Christ, they shouldn't be offered Christ. Both positions sound logical, but neither is. The fallacy becomes obvious if you apply it to the commandments. Men cannot obey God's law perfectly. Does that mean that they don't have to? Is our inability an excuse? Of course not!

The difficulty is resolved by remembering, in the first case, that man is responsible for his own sinful inability and, in the second, that God uses the very commanding and offering to work the miracle of repentance and faith in the hearer. Preachers often, and rightly, refer at this point to our Lord's command to the paralysed man to stretch out his arm. He couldn't, but he did! The power accompanied the command.

Do you remember asking me about 'Pelagianism' and 'duty-faith', which your colleague mentioned? Well, Pelagius was a fourth-century monk who advocated this idea of free will and was condemned, eventually, by the church. The opposite extreme from that is hyper-Calvinism, which says that you cannot command men

Is our inability an excuse?

to repent or believe, i. e. they have no *duty* to have faith. Strangely, the two extremes make the same mistake of equating responsibility with ability. But I am straying from our subject.

What we have here is the old schoolmaster's distinction between 'can' and 'may'. The child who asks, incorrectly, 'Can I leave the room?' is told that he 'can' but that he 'may' not. The sinner 'may' come to Christ, but he 'can' not, unless and until the Lord enables him to do so. Although this is so simple many people do not grasp it. For instance, even editors of hymn-books have been known to slip up. One book has altered the hymn, 'To God be the glory', obviously for this very reason. In the first verse Christ is said to have

> ... opened the life-gate
> That all *may* go in.

This has been altered to 'that *we* may go in'. Now 'all *can* go in' would be wrong, but 'may' is correct—and very important.

No flattery

The other error is to flatter men and abase God in the manner you describe so clearly as happening at the local crusade. God is made to grovel, as it were, in the dust, pleading impotently before men. He can do nothing for them unless they let him, they are told, and so their pride and confidence in themselves are boosted instead of their being humbled before the living God.

I have no objection to evangelists using

The sinner 'may' come to Christ, but he 'can' not, unless and until the Lord enables him to do so.

Revelation 3:20 — 'Here I am! [AV, 'Behold'] I stand at the door and knock. If anyone hears my voice, and opens the door, I will come in and eat with him, and he with me' — to invite unbelievers to Christ. What I do object to is the use of Holman Hunt's picture of this, *The light of the world*, with the stress on the fact that the door has no handle on the outside, so that Christ cannot enter unless he is let in. The true picture is that men *must* let Christ in, but that it is only when God works in them that they *can* do so. Until he provides it, there isn't a handle on the inside either!

On the other hand, we need not continually harp on this. Sometimes, as Christ did with Nicodemus, we need to make man's inability clear, so as to humble him and bring him down from his perch. Usually, however, we must simply tell men that they must repent and must turn and must believe, and that if they do, they may be assured of a welcome from the Saviour. This is not the same as giving them the idea that God is helpless and powerless before them!

I don't suppose that this solves all your problems. In fact, I suspect that it will have raised some that you hadn't even thought of! However, I will try to answer any more you feel like raising. One thing, however, I can tell you. Worship and reverence, the fear of the Lord, which is the beginning of wisdom, and a humble acceptance of the greatness of God and our own smallness are of more use for understanding these issues than any amount of arguments or philosophizing. I'm not suggesting that

Worship and reverence, the fear of the Lord, and a humble acceptance of the greatness of God ... are of more use for understanding these issues than any amount of arguments or philosophizing.

you stop thinking, but that you take care to have the right attitude.

Go on witnessing, even though you will often be discouraged as you face the blindness and hardness of men's hearts. (I sometimes think that people who don't believe in man's inability and bondage have never tried door-to-door work!) Positively, trust a gracious God to make your efforts effective by his Spirit. Many years ago, after speaking about God's sovereignty, I was asked why I bothered preaching. My answer was that the biblical doctrine of man in sin is so dark that it was only belief in God's sovereign working that kept me going at all!

Yours in the bonds of the gospel,

Uncle Harry

Go on witnessing and trust a gracious God to make your efforts effective by his Spirit.

3.

No conditions

My dear Tom,

I was pleased to have your letter, as well as your phone-call — if only to prove that we were still on speaking terms! Now that you have calmed down a bit we can discuss the issues you raised in a temperate and Christian manner.

I'm always amazed — though I suppose I should be used to it by now — at the way Christian people get so worked up at the mere mention of the words 'elect' and 'predestination', as you have done. After all, they do occur in the Bible, so it really isn't on to say we don't believe in them, as so many do! The real question, of course, is 'What do they mean?' followed by, 'What benefit can we derive from them?'

Anyone or no one?

You didn't object to what I wrote last time about man's helpless state as a sinner, so let's start from there. If a man cannot and will not turn from his sin, then we have to accept either that no one will be saved or that God has to take the initiative and do the saving. Now this second alternative is clearly the Bible's teaching. God has elected — which simply means 'chosen' — some people to be saved. According to Ephesians 1:4 he did this 'before the creation of the world', before man was even created.

We may be perplexed as to why God did not elect everybody, but the right way to look at the matter is from the other direction: if God had not elected some then nobody at all would have been saved. God could perfectly justly have left us all to rot in our sin. Which would you prefer? In any case we have no right to dictate to God what he ought to do, especially when we realize that we haven't even got all the facts, never mind the wisdom, to enable us to make this kind of judgement. Incidentally, the apostle Paul makes just this point in Romans 9:20: 'But who are you, O man, to talk back to God? "Shall what is formed say to him who formed it, 'Why did you make me like this?'"'

Beware perversions

At this point the friend you mentioned would no doubt say something like, 'So the elect will be saved whatever they do and if you're not elect you can't be saved, however much you want to be, however much you try. That's not fair.' In fact, John Wesley — great man though he was in other ways — twisted the teaching like

> *We have no right to dictate to God what he ought to do.*

that to make it sound ridiculous. He very naughtily put some words into the mouth of one of his opponents, Augustus Toplady (the one who wrote 'Rock of Ages', but who was himself something of a vitriolic controversialist): 'The sum of it all is this: One in twenty (suppose) of mankind are elected; nineteen are reprobated. The elect shall be saved, do what they will; the reprobate shall be damned, do what they can, witness my hand, A——— T———.' This is a very common misrepresentation — including the alleged proportions, suggesting that very few are saved — which shows not only ignorance of what the Bible teaches, but also a lack of ordinary clear thinking.

The first half of the objection is not so much wrong as plain impossible! The God who chooses an individual to be saved also chooses the way he will be saved, i.e. not just that he will have eternal life, but also that he will have that life through faith in Christ *leading to holiness*. Just take another look at Ephesians 1:4: '... he chose ... to be holy and blameless in his sight'. To put it technically, he ordains the means — repentance, faith and obedience — as well as the end — salvation, or, if you like, not only the terminus, but also all the stations along the line.

This is known as predestination or foreordination; what God has planned is certain to happen, since he brings it about by his providence and especially by the work of his Holy Spirit. So it is not possible for the elect to be saved in unbelief or unholiness, i. e. 'whatever they do', as your friend misrepresents it. There are

God ordains the means as well as the end.

always, of course, those who claim to be elect while their lives give no evidence at all that God has worked in them. Such are self-deceived or quite simply liars. We'll come back to this later.

Now for the other half of your friend's objection. Have you got a vision before your mind's eye of lots of men and women desperately wanting to be saved and God saying, 'I'm sorry you can't come in because you are not elect'? I hope you won't be offended if I say that's plain daft! Remember what I said in my last letter: men and women are so enslaved in sin that they don't, won't and can't come to God to be saved, not truly. If they do come and come in the right way, then it's because God has worked in them by his Spirit, and if he works in them by the Spirit, it's because they are elect. And when they come to God like that he receives them.

Look at it this way

It may seem hard to put it like this, but just think about it for a moment: in the end, nobody who is lost will want to be elect with all that it implies of repentance, faith, submission, obedience and taking up their cross, (as distinct from merely not wanting to go to hell), and nobody who wants to believe, in the biblical sense, will be found not to be elect. Everybody, in fact, has what he wants!

The right way to look at the subject, then, is to say, 'How amazing it is that God, instead of just leaving us all to perish,

> *Nobody who is lost will want to be elect and nobody who wants to believe will be found not to be elect. Everybody, in fact, has what he wants!*

chose a people for himself, to be born
again, repent and believe, and so be saved!'
If you ask me, 'Why not all?' then I have to
admit that I don't know, except that there
are hints in Romans 9:22 about 'God choosing to show his wrath and make his power
known', as well as his mercy, but this is
never really spelled out anywhere. As
usual the Bible concentrates on the positive. That is why so little is said about the
non-elect, the 'reprobate', as they have
been referred to historically — as in the
passage from Wesley quoted earlier.

Reprobation

In fact, some have tried to deny that anyone is reprobate — not as universalists,
denying that anyone is lost, but rather
arguing that the idea of reprobation is
unscriptural logic-chopping ('Since some
are chosen, there must be others who are
rejected') and recoiling in horror from so-
called 'double predestination'. The reason
behind this strange idea — that God chose
some, but made no decision about others
— comes from a very understandable, but
utterly confused, notion that reprobation
means that people are sentenced to eternal
damnation merely because God wills it.
This picture of an arbitrary and very cruel
God, who hurts people and punishes them
everlastingly just because he feels like it, in
a quite arbitrary manner, is naturally re-
pulsive to ordinary decent human beings.
But that is not what I am saying! Nor has it
been the teaching of the church down the
centuries.

*The Bible
concentrates
on the
positive.*

Sovereignty and justice

Now if you would care to look up that copy of the Westminster Confession that I sent you, chapter 3, section VII, you will see what I mean. (I hope you have at least begun to read it; it is the best statement of the truths of Scripture in the English language and perhaps in any language, although my rather limited linguistic gifts forbid me to pronounce certainly on this!) The seventeenth-century authors state the case with great precision — far greater than that used by many who mean to follow them today. They distinguish between the sovereignty, by which God 'passes by' the non-elect, and the justice, by which he ordains that they should be punished *for their sin*. We must never reverse this. Sovereignty alone cannot be the reason for their punishment, because that would pay no respect to sin, and so would be unjust and unfair, and God is righteous. On the other hand, if justice were the reason for not choosing, then God would have to reject us all, because we are all sinners. Keep the distinction clear and, while you won't understand everything, any more than I do, at least you won't be accusing the Lord of injustice or mistakenly denying his sovereignty.

If justice were the reason for not choosing, then God would have to reject us all.

Conditional or unconditional?

You did mention that your friend, when pressed to admit that the Bible does speak of election, muttered something about 'conditional election' — as opposed to 'unconditional', which is what I've been talking about. I'm not surprised that you are puzzled by this; it's a most peculiar idea, a sort of get-out, which enables people to say they believe in election, while in fact, they deny the sovereignty of God.

The idea is this: God, who foresees everything, foresaw that some people would believe (using their supposed free will), so he chose them to be his, with a sort of pre-emptive strike! — i. e. he chose them on the foreseen condition that they would repent and believe. He chose them because he foresaw that they would choose him.

This, of course, makes nonsense of God's choosing. He merely fits in with what man does. It's as ridiculous as the story I once saw — I forget where — of a stranger who rode into a town in the Wild West. At the side of the trail he saw a row of targets painted on the fence-posts, each with a bullet-hole through the bull's-eye. Most impressive shooting! When he got into the town he enquired who the marksman was and was informed, to his astonishment, that he was the town idiot! What he didn't realize was that the man had fired the shots first and then painted the targets in afterwards. He made the target fit the shot, just, so it is alleged, as God makes his election fit man's free choice.

All this, of course, contradicts John 15:16: 'You did not choose me, but I chose you,' as well as the teaching found throughout Scripture, that repentance and faith are the *results* of God's choosing, not the cause of it. Because he has chosen these

Repentance and faith are the results of God's choosing, not the cause of it.

enslaved sinners to be saved, he enables them to believe. Apart from his choice and gracious activity there would be no faith to foresee! Look up, for example, 2 Thessalonians 2:13: 'From the beginning God chose you to be saved through the sanctifying work of the Spirit and through belief in the truth.'

Foreknowledge

Your friend would, no doubt, reply by referring to the mention of God's foreknowledge in Romans 8:29 and 1 Peter 1:2, so just have a careful look at these verses. They do not say that God foresaw that something would happen; they say he foreknew some individuals. Thus Romans 8:29 repeats the word 'those' — those who were foreknown = those were predestined = those who were called etc. Instead of a kind of crystal ball situation, we have a personal relationship, which was established before time. God foreknows *about* everybody, but he knows beforehand, in this personal sense, only some.

Further, as you are aware, the word 'know' in the Bible has a very strong meaning — a dynamic one — more or less equivalent to love. Thus it is used of a man's sexual knowledge of his wife, (e.g. Matthew 1:25 AV — NIV 'had no union') and in Amos 3:2 the NIV actually translates the word (correctly) as 'chosen'. Thus, 'Those God foreknew he also predestined' in Romans 8:29 is more or less the same as 'In love he predestined us' in Ephesians

Have a careful look at Romans 8:29 and 1 Peter 1:2.

1:4-5. We have no cause to be embarrassed by the word 'foreknow'; on the contrary, the thought that God knew me, loved me and took me for his own even before the foundation of the world fills me with 'wonder, love and praise'.

Nations and individuals

The objection is frequently made that God's election is only of nations, not of individuals. The basis for this is thought to be found in Romans 9:13, where the apostle, quoting from Malachi, speaks of God loving Jacob and hating Esau. Now Malachi certainly had nations in mind, and we need have no hesitation in accepting that this is true; but if we look a little further into the matter we see that his statement about the nations is based on God's attitude to the individuals from whom those nations derived. Paul certainly has people in mind, for his argument in Romans 9-11 is that, even though the nation of Israel as a whole has not believed (9:6), some individuals, such as himself, have done so — 'a remnant chosen by grace' (11:5). ('Loved' and 'hated' as used here simply refer to choosing and rejecting.)

Another form of this argument is the assertion that God chose, not for salvation, but for service, as with the nation of Israel. Now it is certainly true that those whom God has chosen are called to serve him, but I cannot see why this should be thought to rule out election to salvation. Indeed, is it not natural that those whom God has

The thought that God knew me, loved me and took me for his own even before the foundation of the world fills me with 'wonder, love and praise'.

chosen for salvation should serve him gladly and with all their hearts?

Finding the evidence

I said I would come back to the matter of God's choosing us to believe and be holy. This is an important practical point and may be of help to those people who came to your church's mission and said they couldn't believe unless they knew they were elect. 'A little knowledge is a dangerous thing,' and I wonder who set them off on this tack. The answer to such people is quite simple, although it is very difficult to reason with them once they've got it into their heads that this is not fair.

Since election leads to faith, faith is the evidence that we are elect. Only those who believe, and prove the genuineness of their faith by its fruit in a changed life, can know they are elect. You can only argue backwards. The order is hear, believe, live for God and then you may draw the deduction that you are God's elect. Only then can you take to yourself all the scriptural comfort and assurance for your future perseverance — and go down on your knees in humble thankfulness and adoration.

Preaching Christ freely

This also disposes of the other alleged problem — that if we believe in election, then we can't truly preach the gospel, because it is all fixed anyway, so we are

The order is hear, believe, live for God and then you may draw the deduction that you are God's elect.

wasting our time. Such an objection completely overlooks one very simple fact: we do not know who these elect are until they believe and are changed. So, knowing that God's purpose includes not only the end but also the means, we go on proclaiming the good news, trusting that God will use our efforts (and our prayers and our compassion and our zeal) to call out his elect from the world.

The same applies at the other end of the spectrum — to those who demand that we should offer Christ only to the elect. Spurgeon was once rebuked for preaching Christ too freely and responded by offering to preach the gospel only to the elect — if his critic would go round first and mark them with a chalk cross! The gospel is for all, not just for those who give evidence that they are elect by being convicted of sin. Such tests of election are bound to fail, since many appear to be convicted, who subsequently do not believe, and others, who may be elect, are discouraged from coming to Christ because they do not know whether they are 'convicted enough'.

By the same token, of course, you can't know that you are not elect, so the folk at your church (we seem to have come a long way from them!) should stop worrying about it and obey the gospel command to repent and put their trust in Christ.

The same kind of argument applies to those who, in every age, have claimed to be elect with no evidence of holiness in their lives. God's election is *to* holiness and no one may claim to belong to the Lord's chosen people unless he is holy.

*The gospel
is
for all.*

Practical importance

The importance of all this should be clear by now. Even apart from the vital matter, which is largely ignored today, of giving God the glory for our salvation, as is his due, this doctrine is a great incentive to holiness. Notice how the apostle Paul, in Colossians 3:12, urges his readers to clothe themselves with all kinds of Christian graces, because they are 'God's chosen people, holy and dearly loved'.

Similarly, the fact that God has chosen us is a great point of assurance since his purpose cannot fail. We can make nothing of the great promises of John 6 and 10 unless we know about election. For instance, the assurance in John 6:37 that Christ will never drive away those who come to him rests on the fact that 'All that the Father gives me [i.e. the elect] will come to me.' Again, the reason why we can take comfort from the fact that no one can snatch us out of the Good Shepherd's hand (John 10:28) is that these are the sheep that the Father has 'given' to him — i. e. the elect yet again.

Here, perhaps more than anywhere else, it is dangerous to argue about the teaching merely theoretically. We must, of course, apply our minds to the Scriptures in reliance on the Holy Spirit, but when we have done all we can to understand, we shall still have to say from the depths of our being, 'Why me, Lord? Why me?' This is not the same as refusing to think at all, because we cannot plumb the depths — the excuse sometimes offered by those

This doctrine is a great incentive to holiness and a great point of assurance.

who do not want to find the answer! Only those who have followed Scripture where it leads and as far as it leads have any right to say, 'I can go no further. I will simply worship and adore.'

Next question, please! I'm quite enjoying this. I hope you're finding it as profitable as I'm finding it stimulating.

Yours affectionately in Christ,

Uncle Harry

Only those who have followed Scripture where it leads and as far as it leads have any right to say, 'I can go no further.'

4.

All the ransomed church of God

My dear Tom,

I was most relieved to hear from you at last. I was beginning to think I had really offended you, so I was pleased to know that you had merely been away on holiday! It was even better to know that you had made use of the time to do some reading — even if only of book reviews. As you say, that can often mean that you need not read the book! However, don't take it too far.

Now, to the problem these reviews raised in your mind. I remember seeing the one you mention, which complained of 'the absence of any discussion of the extent of the atonement'. I wondered at the time what some people would make of that comment. In fact, the subject it refers to is a very important one, so I'll devote this letter to it. It's also very controversial and often simply ignored, even by theologians. I remember, when I was at theological college, of all places, we students could not get a straight answer on this issue. The lecturer on the work of Christ, who should have dealt with it, said nothing about it and, when asked, simply referred us to the principal — presumably lest he got into trouble, either for disagreeing with him, or perhaps just for airing the subject at all. However, the principal just referred us back again to the lecturer, so we got nowhere. Thus many ministers have never even heard of the doctrine I am putting forward. It is completely out of step with current ideas — even among evangelicals — so fasten your seat-belt!

For whom did Christ die?

The question you have raised so tactfully can be put bluntly like this: 'Did Christ die for every single sinner in the world or only for the elect?' Put another way, you can ask, 'Will anyone for whom Christ died go to hell?' (You see how vital the subject is?)

We may approach the subject from either of two directions. Your friend Dick — I like the sound of him; he appears to have his head screwed on right doctrinally, although he may have stated his case rather harshly — has taken the logical and theological approach. That is, if God had already chosen who was to be saved before Christ came into the world, as we saw last time is the case, then he would send Christ to die only for those elect persons, just as he later sent the Holy Spirit to give the new birth to those same people. Thus the three persons of the Trinity have a single and united purpose of salvation, as one would expect. Otherwise, we have the peculiar position where the Son redeems those

> *Did Christ die for every single sinner in the world or only for the elect?*

whom the Father has no intention of saving and the Holy Spirit has no intention of bringing into the kingdom. The other strictly logical point, of course, is that it is inconceivable that God's work should fail, that his intention in Christ's death should be thwarted. But more of that later.

It is inconceivable that God's work should fail.

Effective substitute

In fact that kind of mix-up is impossible, not simply because God would not do that sort of thing, but also because Christ's death is a real substitution, so that the sins have actually been paid for and cannot again be brought into the reckoning. An irreversible work has been done. In addition, the work of the Spirit has been secured, so the link between the different parts of our redemption is not just one of intention, but one of effectiveness. God's justice has actually been satisfied on our behalf, that is, for all whose place Christ took. That is what I mean by a real substitution. Something happened for certain particular people (hence this doctrine is properly called 'particular redemption') when Christ died on the cross; sin was actually punished and paid for; a salvation was actually secured, not just made possible.

If that approach seems cold and hard, just go and sing a few hymns and think about what you are singing — and have sung often already. I know that one of your minister's favourite hymns is 'From whence this fear and unbelief?' by

Augustus Toplady. (Remember him and his debate with John Wesley?) The third verse goes like this:

> If thou hast my discharge procured,
> And freely in my room endured
> The whole of wrath divine;
> Payment God cannot twice demand,
> First at my bleeding Surety's hand,
> And then again at mine.

You see the point, I hope. The payment is real and final, not just if I later believe. Rather the later believing is secured by the payment. See Galatians 3:14: 'He redeemed us ... so that by faith we might receive the promise of the Spirit.' The devil cannot keep me imprisoned when my debt has been paid, any more than Christ could be kept imprisoned by death, once he had finished paying the price.

If Toplady has too controversial a reputation, try William Cowper's ever popular 'There is a fountain filled with blood' (again verse 3):

> Dear dying Lamb, thy precious blood
> Shall never lose its power,
> Till all the ransomed church of God
> Be saved to sin no more.

The same argument applies here: Christ's death has power to free us from bondage, so that we may believe and receive forgiveness (not to procure forgiveness for those who can free themselves).

The payment is real and final.

The biblical approach

The other approach deals directly with the Scriptures, rather than by deduction from other doctrines. You can trace God's purpose right from the beginning. For instance the Passover lamb was provided for the Israelites, God's own people, not for the Egyptians. The sacrifices of the Day of Atonement were for his people only, as were all the rest of the Levitical sacrifices. Or you can refer to specific texts like, 'For the transgression of *my people* he was stricken' (Isaiah 53:8); or 'He will save *his people* from their sins' (Matthew 1:21). Other scriptures describe him as dying for the church (Acts 20:28; Ephesians 5:25); or for his sheep (John 10). What could be clearer than 'I lay down my life for the sheep' (John 10:15), followed by 'You do not believe because you are not my sheep. My sheep listen to my voice; I know them, and they follow me. I give them eternal life and they shall never perish'? (verses 26-28). This is the positive biblical teaching.

You can trace God's purpose right from the beginning.

The other side

Opponents of this doctrine—and they are many and fierce! — will also, of course, quote texts, like the ones you had thrown at you — verses which refer to the world, such as John 3:16 (although that doesn't actually say Christ *died* for the world), and 1 John 2:2 ('the *whole* world'), or which speak of Christ dying for 'all' (e. g. 2 Corinthians 5:14-15) and Hebrews 2:9

which mentions 'everyone'. So they argue, Christ must have died for every single person in the world. And they can quote hymns too — Wesley, of course! His 'O for a thousand tongues ... !' sometimes includes this verse:

> See all your sins on Jesus laid;
> The Lamb of God was slain,
> His soul was once an offering made
> For every soul of man.

Now it is perfectly possible to go through these texts and show that they are all actually consistent with what I have been saying. For instance 'world' often means 'people in general' as in, 'Look, how the whole world has gone after him!' in John 12:19. 'All' can refer to 'all kinds of people', including rulers and Gentiles, as in 1 Timothy 2:1-7, or to 'all nations' as in 'I ... will draw all men to myself' (John 12:32). Frequently, of course, it means 'all of us Christians' or 'all in Christ' (1 Corinthians 15:22), or 'all the people I've been referring to', as in Hebrews 2:9 and 2 Corinthians 5:14-15. Just think of the implications if we took Colossians 1:23 literally and asserted that the gospel 'has been proclaimed to every creature under heaven'!

Even worse, such an interpretation would prove too much. It would mean not just that Christ had made salvation possible for all, although they would not all enjoy it, but that all would be saved. See 1 Corinthians 15:22: 'For as in Adam all die, so in Christ all will be made alive.' Again, 2 Corinthians 5:19 tells us that 'God was reconciling *the world* to himself in Christ',

Just think of the implications if we took Colossians 1:23 literally and asserted that the gospel 'has been proclaimed to every creature under heaven'!

but this cannot mean making reconciliation possible for every single person in the world, for it continues, 'not counting men's sins against them'. Taking 'world' in the sense that some people want to would have to mean that everybody was, in fact, forgiven! Now I am sure that your friends are not universalists in that sense, but they have to face up to this.

Practical implications

All this, however, will just seem so much special pleading or mere theological hair-splitting to your earnest, evangelistically-minded friends. They are so concerned with the implications for evangelism that they are impatient with our arguments. They do not so much reject them as refuse to think about them. Now, I have much sympathy with their motives and their longing to have sinners saved — I want this just as much — but the question is whether what we are saying and doing is really according to God's Word and, therefore, in line for his approval and blessing. So we must take the time and trouble to think.

    I remember friends in my youth challenging me, just as yours have done, 'If Christ did not die for everyone, but only for the elect, how can you preach the gospel to them? You can't tell them to believe that Christ died for them.' In fact, they would assert very strongly that anyone who believes in 'particular redemption', which they would call 'limited atonement', cannot really preach the gospel freely.

The question is whether what we are saying and doing is really according to God's Word.

Now, if that were true, it would be quite devastating, for I certainly want to preach the gospel to everyone without exception. It all seems crushingly logical, until you query the basic presupposition. Ask yourself the simple question: 'Where in the Bible is any unbeliever told to believe that Christ died for him?' In spite of multitudes of tracts and booklets which specify that the way to be saved is to believe just that, the answer is, 'Nowhere'!

True gospel preaching

Now, I'm sorry if that upsets your apple-cart and means that you have to start again from scratch, learning how to preach the gospel biblically, but really this is most important. I sometimes wonder whether the basic reason for insisting on particular redemption is so that we preach the gospel properly. Perhaps not; the ultimate reason must be the glory of God, for denying particular redemption reflects most adversely on his wisdom, power, grace and justice, as I've tried to indicate earlier. Nevertheless, it seems to me that because preachers make such an effort, and think it is enough, to tell sinners that Christ died for them, they fail to do what is most important — to tell them to repent and trust Christ personally.

The apostles told their hearers to 'Repent … and turn to God' (Acts 3:19), and to 'Believe in the Lord Jesus' (Acts 16:31), with no suggestion that they ought to concentrate on believing, as a fact, that Jesus had died for them. The Lord himself

> *Where in the Bible is any unbeliever told to believe that Christ died for him?*

did not tell his hearers to believe that he would die for them. He said, 'Come to *me*.'

Jesus did tell his disciples at the Last Supper that the bread represented his body which was given for them specifically, but he did not say this to all his hearers in general. The debate about whether those words were said to and about Judas is irrelevant, as is the issue of whether he shared in the first Lord's Supper. At that point Jesus was clearly treating him as a professed believer, which was how the other disciples obviously regarded him. Our Lord's knowledge of his treachery was supernatural and not something we can emulate.

Preaching faith in Christ

Please don't misunderstand me. I'm not saying you must not or cannot preach the gospel freely to all men, nor am I saying that you cannot tell everyone to repent and believe. I am simply saying, 'Don't tell people that Christ died for them.' What the New Testament does is quite different, although many people don't seem able to grasp it. The apostles told their hearers, not to believe *that*, but to believe *in*. They did not tell them to believe that Christ died for them; they exhorted them to believe *in* Christ and to trust *him alone* for salvation. The important thing is to put your trust in Christ himself, to rest upon him, rely upon him personally, not just believe certain things about him. Then he will save you, through his death on the cross.

You can believe Christ died for you

You can believe Christ died for you and still go to hell, but if you put your trust in him, nothing can harm you.

and still go to hell, but if you put your trust in him, nothing can harm you. You can believe Christ died for you and go on living in ungodliness, but faith in Christ leads to a new life in his service.

Of course, we do have to believe certain things about him — and about ourselves: our need, our guilt, our condemnation, and his deity, humanity and power and willingness to save all who come to him. But faith itself is committing ourselves to him; it is not just believing that he can or that he did or *'that'* anything. We have to come to *him*.

No need for bondage

I'm afraid that some preachers, who have come to believe the orthodox doctrine in a vacuum, as it were, have then begun to tie themselves in knots trying to preach the gospel, without actually telling people that Christ died for them. They spend so much thought and energy avoiding that and trying instead to say, 'Christ died for sinners,' that they lose all their liberty and end up hardly preaching anything.

But once you see the biblical pattern you can aim positively at calling upon them to trust in Christ, the Saviour. First you explain how Christ saves his people by his death on the cross and then, without any restriction, you urge them with warmth and earnestness to repent towards God and put their trust in Christ. I am most grateful to Dr Jim Packer, who years ago pointed all this out before a Christian Union mission at London University. It

Once you see the biblical pattern you can aim positively at calling upon people to trust in Christ, the Saviour.

later went into print in his book, *Evangelism and the Sovereignty of God*.

Christ and him crucified

In fact, I think we can go a stage further than I have outlined above — if we are careful. A group of Scottish ministers in the eighteenth century, known as the 'Marrow Men', used to use the expression, 'Christ is dead for you', (which is not the same as 'Christ died for you'). I think that this expression is itself rather liable to misunderstanding, but the point they were making is vital. It is the crucified Lord whom we set before sinners — a Saviour with a salvation. We must not slip into suggesting that Christ did not die for them! We can never say that. What they need to know is that this Saviour was crucified for sinners and that all the benefits of that cross are theirs if they come to him.

I wonder really if that is what the apostle John was saying in 1 John 2:2 (I much prefer the AV here): 'And he is the propitiation for our sins: and not for ours only, but also for the sins of the whole world.' We can explain 'the whole world' as meaning Gentiles as well as Jews, but to many people that seems less convincing here than elsewhere. What if John is saying the same as the Marrow Men? He does not say that Christ *made* a propitiation for the sins of the whole world, but that he *is* the propitiation for them. Just as Christ is set before men as 'the Saviour of the world' (1 John 4:14; John 4:42), that is, not that he saves the whole world, but that anyone

It is the crucified Lord whom we set before sinners — a Saviour with a salvation.

who wants a Saviour must come to him, so here, anyone in the whole world who wants a propitiation for his sins must come to him. *He* is the only and all-sufficient propitiation. That is only a suggestion, but what is clear is that we must set Christ crucified before men, a powerful Saviour who has all that is necessary to save those who come to him.

Limited atonement

Just one last point. So much depends on how doctrines are presented. You can put this teaching forward in a hard cold manner, which gives the impression to fellow-Christians, not to mention unbelievers, that they are excluded from God's mercy. I want to stress two positive things. The first is that preaching the gospel in the way I have been explaining is a better way than the modern one — in fact, it is the only true and biblical way. It is more likely, not less, to produce *genuine* converts.

The other matter is this. I want to stress the wonder and effectiveness of Christ's death for sinners, as in the hymns I quoted earlier. You can either limit the scope of Christ's death or limit its effectiveness. (You cannot have an atonement which is both effective and universal without falling into universalism.) You can either have a narrow bridge which goes right across the abyss or a wide one, which stops half-way. I know which I prefer — and which is in accordance with the Scriptures. Use the word 'limited' when you need to, but stress the effectiveness.

You can either have a narrow bridge which goes right across the abyss or a wide one, which stops half-way.

I hope this hasn't shaken you too much and that you will think seriously about it. It really is the historic, orthodox doctrine and it still matters.

Yours in the bonds of the gospel,

Uncle Harry

I hope that you will think seriously about this. It is the historic, orthodox doctrine, and it still matters.

5.

Unconquerable grace

My dear Tom,

I thought it must be my birthday when your parcel arrived the other day! It was certainly a wonderful present to read your letter enthusing about the doctrines of grace. Thank you, too, for the booklets in the parcel which you sent me for my comment. Before I respond to that request, I ought to comment on something else. I'm a little troubled by your assumption that 'Everybody believes in grace.' Professor Joad was before your time — and very nearly before mine — but he became very well known for saying on the BBC's *Brains Trust* programme (steam radio, of course!), 'Well, it all depends what you mean by ... ' We, too, have to ask what people mean by 'grace'. Is it really sovereign grace? And even that has to be defined.

Defining our terms

The trouble today is that even those who deny the most basic doctrines of the faith want to be regarded as orthodox. They want to keep the aura of respectability that attaches to the great words that have been used in the church. So they use Bibles in their pulpits; they have texts for their sermons and they insist that they believe in, for example, the resurrection — 'although not in a crude literal sense'! Thus they feel able to assert the traditional doctrines, having first evacuated them of all meaning. Now the people we are considering are not in that category, but they do follow the same practice to some extent. We have already seen this in their treatment of 'election'. Similarly, they cannot avoid the word 'grace', so, in order to avoid the doctrine they redefine the meaning of the word or at least its application.

> *'Well, it all depends what you mean by...'*

Grace means 'unmerited favour', but the outworking of that, which is what we are actually concerned with, is that God chose some in his grace, Christ died for them in his grace and the Holy Spirit applied that salvation to them in *his* grace, so that 'Salvation is from the Lord,' from beginning to end. Grace applies to the whole work, not just to the issue of works or faith. And that brings me to your booklets, or rather to one in particular.

Misleading titles

You will have gathered by now, if you didn't know it already, that I agree wholeheartedly with the contents of the booklets, but I do have reservations about one of the titles: *Irresistible grace*. Unless it is qualified and explained very carefully,

this term can be very misleading and it
has, in fact, been used to cast doubt on the
whole doctrine. It makes the whole process
of conversion sound automatic and
mechanical, taking no account of the
doubts and fears, the perplexities and
hesitations, the struggles of counting the
cost, the arguments and counter-
arguments, which often precede coming
to Christ. It can give the impression that it
doesn't matter whether we witness or not,
whether we persuade and plead or not,
because the Spirit will get his way by
riding roughshod over intellect, feelings
and will, 'compelling' people to believe in
a most ungracious and even artificial way.

So the term 'irresistible', though
accurate in the sense that the Holy Spirit's
sovereign purpose is never defeated,
should be avoided. This is all the more
important as opponents only have to refer
to Acts 7:51 — 'You always resist the Holy
Spirit!' — to show that we are wrong, as far
as the unsophisticated believer is
concerned.

As well as the resistance which the
unbeliever puts up on the way to
repentance and faith, it would seem that
there is also a work of the Spirit which
does not result, and is not intended to
result, in conversion. Men fight against
conviction of sin and it wears off; they
count the cost and decide that the price is
too high. All this, *in a sense*, resists the
grace of God in the gospel. That is one
reason why we must never stop short of
urging men to put their faith in Christ.
Conviction and seeking are not enough.

On the other hand, when the Spirit

> *We must never
> stop short
> of urging men
> to put their
> faith in Christ.
> Conviction
> and seeking
> are not
> enough.*

works in the elect, he renews their minds, hearts and wills, so that, however long it may take, they do willingly and deliberately turn from their sins to God. A better term would be 'invincible' — if only people knew what it meant, i. e. unconquerable.

Gifts of God

You will find this teaching everywhere in the New Testament, especially in the references to calling and the new birth. There are verses which tell us that repentance and faith are God's gift, the outworking of his purpose, (not the reason for his choice, as in 'conditional election'). In Philippians 1:29 Paul tells his readers that 'It has been *granted* to you on behalf of Christ not only to believe on him but also to suffer for him', while Acts 11:18 says the same about 'repentance unto life'. Further on, Acts 13:48 says that 'All who were appointed for eternal life believed.'

Ephesians 2:8-9 perhaps demands a little more comment. You remember the text, I'm sure: 'For it is by grace you have been saved, through faith — and this not from yourselves, it is the gift of God — not by works, so that no one can boast.' This is often quoted as proof that faith is the gift of God — and, indeed, most translations read as if this is so. In fact, they can hardly do anything else in the circumstances. However, the reality is not quite that simple. The difficulty is grammatical and I'm not sure how good your grammar is! The Greek for 'this' (being neuter) cannot refer back either to faith or to grace (which are femi-

Repentance and faith are God's gift.

nine), so we have to refer it to the whole process of salvation which Paul has been describing. However, although this does not specifically say that faith is a gift of God, faith is certainly included in the whole, which *is* a gift of God. You may wonder why we have to go into it like this, if the end result is the same. The reason is so that it is quite clear, even to our opponents, that we are subject only to the Word of God.

Drawn by the Father

John's Gospel is full of this teaching, especially chapter 6. Verse 37 has always been a favourite with those who insist both on God's sovereignty and man's responsibility, because it teaches first that all the elect — 'all that the Father gives me' — will come to Christ, and then that no one who comes will be rejected. What a marvellous combination of truths! You won't go far wrong if you keep to this balance. Then verse 44 elaborates with the negative: 'No one can come to me unless the Father who sent me draws him,' while verse 45 gives the positive, showing how this works out: 'Everyone who listens to the Father and learns from him comes to me.'

I think Philip Doddridge must have had those verses in mind when he wrote his hymn, 'O happy day that fixed my choice!' Some people have objected to his mention of choice, as if we did not in fact choose God at all! The real position is that the first line states what happened from

John 6:37 has always been a favourite ... You won't go far wrong if you keep to this balance.

our human point of view, while the second verse explains how that came about:

He drew me and I followed on,
Charmed to confess the voice divine.

Another instance which is crucial in the argument is the one which convinced me about all this many years ago — the conversion of Lydia in Acts 16. You remember how several women were listening to the apostle Paul at Philippi, but the Lord singled out Lydia. All heard the words, but only Lydia believed. Why? The answer is given in verse 14: 'The Lord opened her heart to respond to Paul's message.' What could be clearer?

Grace for all?

I didn't notice anything about 'common grace' in your booklets, so perhaps I'd better say something about it, as many people get confused. 'Common' in this expression means shared by everybody, as in 'common land' or 'common parlance', not 'frequent' or 'vulgar', but there's a right use and a wrong use of it. The wrong use, also referred to as 'sufficient grace', is the idea, popularized by John Wesley, that in order to be fair to all God must give everybody the same opportunity to be saved. (It's rather like the Equal Opportunities Commission today!) So, through Christ's death God frees everybody's will — puts it into a sort of neutral position — so that he has the liberty and ability (sufficient grace) to repent and

All heard the words, but only Lydia believed. Why? 'The Lord opened her heart.'

believe, *if he will*. You see how everything depends, in the last analysis, on man's will, which God does nothing about and can do nothing about.

This stress on the will, with the idea of God having to wait and see what man will decide, sounds like many modern preachers, but there is one difference. To be fair to Wesley we must realize that his teaching is not free will in the sense in which Pelagius and Charles G. Finney used it. They regarded this freedom as a natural ability; Wesley does insist that the natural man is a slave and depends on the grace of God to give him this opportunity to believe. Nevertheless, it is still unbiblical and quite different from what I have been saying.

Apart from anything else the whole idea is impossible — you can't be neutral — and in the case of those who never hear the gospel, it is quite pointless, i. e. the whole idea of fairness breaks down unless God ensures that all actually hear the gospel, which is not the case. The Scriptures teach that God gives faith, not the mere possibility of faith. Lydia's heart was opened, not so that she might respond, but so that she would and did respond. You don't hear much of this 'sufficient grace' today, since most people have slipped right back into believing in absolute free will. They are far more unscriptural than Wesley was.

The Scriptures teach that God gives faith, not the mere possibility of faith.

Common grace

Now proper 'common grace' is genuinely grace — free and undeserved — and is truly common — given to all, irrespective of whether they are elect or not — but it stops short of salvation. In this common grace God restrains sin, gives good gifts to all men and even enables unbelievers to live lives that are, in human terms, good. Psalm 145: 9, 17 reads,

> 'The Lord is good to all;
> he has compassion on all he has
>   made ...
> The Lord is righteous in all his ways
> and loving towards all he has made.'

It is probably in this sense of preserving and providing for them that God 'is the Saviour of all men, and especially of those who believe' (1 Timothy 4:10).

There are some who object to the use of the words 'grace' and 'love' in this connection, preferring to reserve these great terms for God's saving grace. However, in Matthew 5:43-45 we are encouraged to behave after the pattern of the Father who 'causes his sun to rise on the evil and the good, and sends rain on the righteous and unrighteous'. This we do by *loving* even our enemies, so the use of the word is justified. Thus there is nothing wrong with telling everybody that God loves them, so long as you and they know what you mean, and provided that you are not denying that they are also under God's wrath. The very fact that they are hearing the gospel is in itself an evidence of God's love and concern for them.

So when we see non-Christians living moral lives, when we find ungodly rulers

There is nothing wrong with telling everybody that God loves them, so long as you and they know what you mean.

governing wisely, when we celebrate amazing scientific and medical discoveries, when we encounter unbelievers unselfishly caring for the old and handicapped in a way that puts us to shame — as we often do — we should not cynically question their motives or try to deny the facts. We should recognize the common grace of God at work in them and be thankful, giving the glory to God, not man. Nor should we doubt what the Bible teaches about sin. Such good works etc. are not the same as righteousness before God; they do not justify a man before him. For salvation these people need the specific and distinguishing, saving grace of God in Christ.

Effectual calling

It occurs to me that, having mentioned 'calling' once at the beginning, I have not referred to it again — an omission that I ought to remedy, since this is one of the most common terms used in the New Testament to describe becoming a Christian. Our forefathers used it a lot too, often referring to it as 'effectual (effective) calling', but it has very much gone out of fashion today, probably because it depends on a view of salvation which begins and ends with God. Nowadays you are much more likely to come across the word used about being called to be a minister or a missionary, or about a man's calling in life. Both of these uses are related to the basic meaning, to which I am referring.

Calling is the work of God, through the

> *Calling is the work of God, through the outward call of the gospel and the inner operations of the Holy Spirit, which causes a man to come to Christ.*

outward call of the gospel and the inner operations of the Holy Spirit, which causes a man to come to Christ. You find our Lord using the word to refer simply to the call or invitation of the gospel in his statement: 'Many are called [NIV, invited] but few are chosen' (Matthew 22:14). However, in the rest of the New Testament 'calling' is used only of those who *are* chosen, as in the great chain of salvation in Romans 8:30: 'And those he predestined, he also called; those he called, he also justified; those he justified, he also glorified.'

In fact, in 1 Corinthians 1:24 the 'called' are distinguished from the rest of humanity and in verses 26 and 27 the character of those who have been called is used to define the character of those who are God's chosen. (The link is similar in 2 Peter 1:10.) Thus, to go back to an earlier example, all the women in Philippi heard the call of the gospel, but only Lydia was called effectually so as to become a Christian.

God saves through the gospel, not independently of it.

The importance of this term is twofold. In the first place it reminds us that God saves through the gospel, not independently of it. In 2 Thessalonians 2:13-14 Paul reminds his readers that though they were chosen 'from the beginning' to be saved, God 'called you to this through our gospel, that you might share in the glory of our Lord Jesus Christ'. The other thing to note is that we are almost invariably said to be called *to* something, e. g. glory, as in the verses just quoted or, especially, holiness: 'For God did not call us to be impure, but to live a holy life' (1 Thessalonians 4:7).

It is about time we reinstated this term, so that it is clearly seen that salvation is at

God's initiative and that his gospel does not just invite (as it does all who hear), but transfer, as it does the elect. There is power in the call of God. 2 Corinthians 4:6 uses the parallel of the light-creating word of Genesis 1 to describe the call, while the creative word of Christ in healing and in raising the dead is used by many a preacher as an illustration of it.

Speaking to the dead

It must have seemed sheer folly for our Lord to address to the dead Lazarus the word of command: 'Come out.' He could not hear or respond — but he did. There was power in the call. It was sheer folly to command the man with the paralysed arm to stretch it out, but there was power in the command. It is sheer folly, to the eyes of man, to address the call to repentance and faith to men who are dead in their sins, but when we do so we find there is power in the gospel. Where God accompanies the words with the power of the Spirit (1 Thessalonians 1:4-5), there follow conviction and salvation.

The other side of this, of course, is that the preacher knows that it is his words that God uses. He cannot go about his business in a couldn't-care-less attitude, but must try to be as clear as possible, as warm as possible and as earnest as possible. While not preaching for decisions, in the modern sense of man-made statistics, he does preach for decision — for conversion. It is here that Paul's words in 2 Corinthians 5:20 are so important. Far from agreeing

There is power in the call of God.

with those who deny that the preacher should 'offer' Christ to unbelievers, still less 'command' all men everywhere to repent (Acts 17:30) and believe (which they stigmatize as 'duty faith'), Paul uses words like 'appeal' and 'implore' to describe his manner of preaching the gospel of reconciliation.

Does it matter?

Knowing you as I do now — which is one of the benefits I've gained from our correspondence — I realize that your next question will be, 'Why does it matter? Of what practical use is this doctrine of invincible grace?' Quite right. And knowing me as you do now, you ought to be able to guess what my answer will be! Yes, of course, the chief reason for asserting this doctrine is the glory of God. On any other view we have to concede the possibility of God's purpose of salvation being thwarted; the elect might not believe; Christ's death for them might prove to be in vain. The same reason appears from another angle. Any other doctrine gives the praise and glory to man — either the one who decides or the one who persuades. The correct position must not only be held, but be seen to be held.

There are, however, other practical consequences of holding to this teaching — as always. Let me ask you a simple question. When you want someone to be saved, to whom do you pray? What a silly question! Of course, you pray to the Lord. You ask him to open the blind eyes, to

When you want someone to be saved, to whom do you pray?

soften the hard heart and bend the stub-
born will. You plead with God to grant
your friend or relative repentance and to
draw him to himself. It does not occur to
you, nor, I'm thankful to say, to most of
those who are confused about the doctrine, to pray to the person himself!

This doctrine, in other words, is our
assurance, when we come up against
people with hearts like rocks, that all is not
lost. We cannot persuade them, but 'What
is impossible with men is possible with
God' (Luke 18:27). When the friend you
witness to about the gospel says, 'You'll
never convert me,' you can say to yourself,
or even to him on occasions, 'No, but God
can!' Men can be changed, from within,
and saved in spite of all their present
opposition. Have you ever sung these
words?

When the friend you witness to about the gospel says, 'You'll never convert me,' you can say, 'No, but God can!'

> Thou canst o'ercome this heart of mine,
> Thou wilt victorious prove;
> For everlasting strength is thine,
> And everlasting love.

> Thy powerful Spirit shall subdue
> Unconquerable sin,
> Cleanse this foul heart, and make it
>   new,
> And write thy law within.

Believe it or not, they were written by
Charles Wesley! Perhaps we should call
the doctrine 'unconquerable grace'.

It is faith in the grace of God which
gives us hope, both of individual conver-
sions and of a new and glorious work of
God in our generation. How, apart from a

sovereign work of God, can we hope for this present evil state of the church and the world to be changed? Why else, indeed, do we call such awakenings and revivals 'a work of God'?

Lastly, this will also make us careful in our evangelism, to use only those methods which have the Holy Spirit's approval (i. e. in the Scriptures), for whatever we may achieve by other means, it is unlikely to be real conversion.

Yours by unconquerable grace,

Uncle Harry

> *It is faith in the grace of God which gives us hope, both of individual conversions and of a new and glorious work of God in our generation.*

6.

Presumption or perseverance

My dear Tom,

Thank you for your recent letter. I really look forward to hearing from you and responding to the challenges you throw down. I'm very impressed with the increasing discernment you are showing and the way you examine doctrinal statements carefully — as we need to do. There is, of course, one drawback to this: I have to be very careful how I express myself! ('Do you good,' I can hear you saying and you may well be right!)

So, for example, you question my statement last time that there is a work of the Holy Spirit which does not lead to conversion. I can assure you it is not heretical and, moreover, it is relevant to our next topic — whether a real Christian can ever be lost. This is the one element in the doctrines of grace which is accepted by many, perhaps most Christians, who would reject the rest, so we need to look at it even more carefully than usual. (There I go again! I really can't complain, can I?)

As you will realize, this all arises from

your draft essay (article? sermon?) on 'Eternal security', which you asked me to comment on. I have read it (critically! How else?) and I'm quite delighted with it — on the whole. (Did I hear a groan? You wouldn't want me to be less vigilant than yourself, would you?) Your statement of the biblical doctrine with the relevant proofs is first class. I especially liked the way you distinguished between the theological arguments, beginning from the fact of God's sovereign plan and showing that this cannot fail to 'bring us safe home', and the simple biblical texts like, 'He who began a good work in you will carry it on to completion until the day of Christ Jesus' (Philippians 1:6); and 'I know whom I have believed, and am convinced that he is able to guard what I have entrusted to him for that day' (2 Timothy 1:12).

Titles again

However, one thing could spoil the whole effect. That is the title — again! 'Eternal security' is an expression which is perfectly all right as long as you understand it properly, but I'm afraid that many people — the unwary, the unlearned and the unspiritual — pervert it into something quite dreadful, 'to their own destruction'. The other expression you use — 'once saved, always saved' — comes into the same category, I'm afraid, and has been abused only too frequently.

The better title, which is the traditional one, is 'the final perseverance of the saints', although even that has its dangers. What

Many people pervert 'eternal security' into something quite dreadful, 'to their own destruction'.

we need, but haven't got, is a label which reflects both the sovereign, keeping power of God and the necessary diligence of man in persevering faith and godliness. This balance is seen perfectly in 1 Peter 1:5, referring to those 'who are kept by the power of God through faith unto salvation ready to be revealed in the last time'. (Yes, I prefer the AV here; it puts the stress on God first, which is vital and final.) Final perseverance can sound as if it all depended on our efforts; eternal security can lead to a false sense of security, as if we played no part in the matter.

The fact is that God does everything and we do everything; he works in us and through us, as you can see in my favourite guide-line text: 'Continue to work out your salvation with fear and trembling, for it is God who works in you to will and to act according to his good purpose' (Philippians 2:12-13 — back to the NIV!).

The danger of presumption

You may ask, 'What is all the fuss about? Surely it's only a matter of emphasis? It could be, but too often it isn't. There are many people who profess to have faith and claim to be saved, but who produce no evidence of this. They go through life attending church, perhaps, and bearing the name of Christian, but they do not grow in grace or make progress in holy living. When they are challenged about this, either personally or through the public preaching of the Word, they reply that they were once saved, so they are always

> *The fact is that God does everything and we do everthing; he works in us and through us.*

saved; that they are Christ's sheep and, therefore, according to John 10:27-29, eternally secure.

The doctrine is true, but the application is dangerously, indeed fatally, faulty. It ignores the fact that there is such a thing as a false profession, a temporary faith, a decision which is not conversion, a moral reformation which is not the new birth. There is a vast difference between saying or thinking you are saved and actually being saved.

This is not just theory — a mere vague possibility. Ministers and others are constantly meeting young people, and older folk, who insist that they are 'all right', because they once made a decision, in spite of the lack of any evidence that they are new creations in Christ. They refuse to examine themselves as to whether they are in the faith — which could lead to their realizing that they are not and so to genuine repentance — and may end their days in a lost condition. While the emphasis on perseverance may produce stress and anxiety if it is not properly presented, at least it does not lead to deadly false security and so I prefer this title and emphasis.

While we are on this aspect of the subject, I ought to explain that there are some who actually teach that we are secure once we have believed, without qualifying that by insisting on a faith that produces works as evidence of its genuineness. 'The person who is saved ... will go to heaven when he dies, no matter what work (or lack of work) may accompany such faith. In other words, no matter what sin (or

There is a vast difference between saying or thinking you are saved and actually being saved.

absence of Christian obedience) may accompany such faith.' (As you will realize, I am actually quoting someone!) The obvious conclusion that many will draw is: 'Believe in Christ and live as you like.'

Unsafe remedies

Now it must readily be conceded that people who teach this, like the author I have just quoted, don't intend that conclusion to be drawn. They are usually very keen on holiness and obedience to the Word of God. This being so, they adopt other methods of trying to secure such holiness and obedience. One method is to place an unbiblical stress on rewards for the Christian, so that salvation itself almost pales into insignificance by comparison, in order to stir people up to greater efforts.

The other method is to describe a person who does not show any evidence of holiness of life or obedience to God, not as a false professor, which is probably the case, but as a 'carnal Christian', and then to urge him to take a second step of entire consecration or full surrender or, more recently, to seek for the baptism of the Spirit, in order to enter upon a higher level of Christian experience. I haven't time to go into all that here — it's not really on the subject — but I am trying to show why it is so important to talk in terms of the perseverance of the saints. Once you depart from the biblical and balanced position, that God's keeping grace operates through our obedient living, you get lost in a wilderness of heretical ideas.

Once you depart from the biblical and balanced position you get lost in a wilderness of heretical ideas.

Definitions

In this connection we need to be able to distinguish things that differ, such as apostasy and backsliding, salvation by works and judgement by works, assurance and presumption. Stop reading for a while and try a few definitions ... Well, how did you get on?

Christians can and do backslide; professing Christians commit apostasy, that is, they give up their profession of faith and are lost, because they never were truly saved. The question is often asked, 'How do we know whether someone is backsliding or apostatizing?' Usually, when someone you thought was a Christian stops coming to church or falls into serious and open sin, you don't know which it is. Fortunately we don't need to know; the remedy is the same in both cases: repentance.

Next, we are not saved by works; to the end of our days our trust must be wholly in the Lord Jesus Christ, in his righteousness and death. Nothing must shift us from this. Nevertheless, we shall be judged by our works — the evidence of the reality of the faith that leads to justification.

Holiness and heaven

We are not saved by our holiness, but we cannot be saved apart from holiness and without holiness, as Hebrews 12:14 makes very clear: 'Make every effort to live in peace with all men and to be holy; without

Stop reading for a while and try a few definitions ...

holiness no one will see the Lord.' We are not forgiven because we forgive others, but unless we forgive others we shall not be forgiven: 'For if you forgive men when they sin against you, your heavenly Father will also forgive you. But if you do not forgive men their sins, your heavenly Father will not forgive your sins' (Matthew 6:14-15).

This is so because a genuine experience of God's mercy will make us merciful, too (Matthew 18:21-35). We are not saved because we evangelize, but unless we evangelize we shall not be saved, because a real experience of the grace of God will lead us to care for others, too: 'I do all this for the sake of the gospel, that I may share in its blessings' (1 Corinthians 9:23 — note the 'I', not 'they').

The same work of the Holy Spirit which produces faith unto justification also produces regeneration unto holiness. So there will never be anybody standing before the judgement seat of Christ who has no works to be taken as evidence of his faith. There are many people who resent any teaching along these lines and insist that if you say this you are preaching salvation by works. Too many try to avoid the implications of Romans 2:6-7, by saying that the apostle is speaking hypothetically, instead of realizing that he is talking of the effects and evidence of genuine faith. It is, therefore, utterly true that 'God "will give to each person according to what he has done". To those who by persistence in doing good seek glory, honour and immortality, he will give eternal life. But for those who are self-seeking and who reject the truth and

We are not saved by our holiness, but we cannot be saved apart from, and without holiness.

follow evil, there will be wrath and anger.'

Don't be put off; it is vital that we insist on the importance of accompanying works. In this way, of course, it will be seen at the last day that God does not condone sin. He who saves us from the guilt and consequences of our sins also saves us from sin itself.

Assurance and presumption

The doctrine of final perseverance is intended to give us a proper assurance of salvation. This means that because we are his now — and have evidence to prove it — the Lord will keep us through all the trials and difficulties that may await us in the future. It is not intended to assure us that in spite of present ungodliness and future carelessness we shall certainly be saved. That is presumption. It may, of course, be the case that people at present living an ungodly life are actually backsliders and are destined for eternal life. However, they have no right to that assurance. This is why the right way to gain assurance, as the Puritans often stressed, is simply to get on with living the Christian life with all diligence.

The strange fact is that there are so many Christians who insist that you can know very definitely that you are a Christian now — as John Wesley did — but then say that you can give all this up and be lost at last! What is the use of an assurance that is here today and gone tomorrow? The biblical stress as far as assurance is concerned is not that I am saved now, but that

The right way to gain assurance is simply to get on with living the Christian life.

I will be kept safe in the future. To put the stress on *now* can lead to resting on my oars and taking everything for granted. The real aim is to help and encourage those who know their own weakness and the power of the evil one, and therefore fear the future.

'What if I have to suffer persecution? What if I encounter great personal disasters? Will my faith hold then?' These are the questions that arise in the humble Christian's mind. The answer of the Scriptures is clear and definite: 'Who shall separate us from the love of Christ? Shall trouble or hardship or persecution or famine or nakedness or danger or sword? As it is written: "For your sake we face death all day long; we are considered as sheep to be slaughtered." No, in all these things we are more than conquerors through him who loved us. For I am convinced that neither death nor life, neither angels nor demons, neither the present nor the future, nor any powers, neither height nor depth, nor anything else in all creation, will be able to separate us from the love of God that is in Christ Jesus our Lord' (Romans 8:35-39).

To me one of the saddest things in modern Christianity is the number of people who will quote these verses, and others like them, and then still say that the Christian can fall from grace and be lost.

'What if I have to suffer persecution? What if I encounter great personal disasters? Will my faith hold then?'

What about Hebrews 6?

In your otherwise excellent survey of the biblical texts bearing on this subject, you skated over one passage that is constantly causing trouble to young Christians — and to some not so young ones. Without doubt, this is the passage that I have had most questions about during my ministry: Hebrews 6:4-6. I sensed that you were rather uneasy when you had to refer to it, so let's have a look at it.

The problem is this, isn't it: these verses seem to assert that it is possible for Christians to fall away so badly that it becomes impossible to bring them to repentance and, in consequence, they are finally lost. Now, in the light of the clear teaching of the rest of Scripture, that cannot be the case. Difficult passages like this one must be interpreted in the light of the clear ones — all of which unequivocally teach that real Christians can never stop being Christians and can never be lost.

Therefore, there are three possibilities: either the people described are not lost, or they are not Christians, or the whole passage is a hypothetical warning, but can't really happen. Some take the first option, arguing that this only refers to losing rewards (or a place in the millennial kingdom!). Few hold to this, as verse 8 seems to speak of hell itself, especially the reference to 'being cursed'. You, I gather, favour the last view, and you are in good company with many sound men, including Spurgeon. There are, of course, many passages which tell us that unless we persevere we shall not be saved.

Colossians 1:22-23 comes into this category: 'But now he has reconciled you by Christ's physical body through death

> *Difficult passages must be interpreted in the light of the clear ones.*

to present you holy in his sight, without blemish and free from accusation — if you continue in your faith, established and firm, not moved from the hope held out in the gospel.'

This is certainly intended to stir us up to persevere, but it is not really hypothetical; it will actually happen that some are lost. If we do not persevere we shall not be saved. There are some who do not persevere, because they are not real believers in the first place, and they will not be saved. In fact, Hebrews 6:11 says the same thing positively: 'We want each of you to show this same diligence to the very end, in order to make your hope sure.'

In such passages the people addressed are not assumed to be Christians; they may or may not be. Time will tell; those who persevere are the true Christians. This, however, should not remove assurance from those who are pursuing a godly course at the moment, only from the presumptuous. Here, in Hebrews 6, however, the people are described in a very detailed way. Such people can be lost. The question is: 'Are they real Christians?'

Time will tell; those who persevere are the true Christians.

The people described

Surely, many say, the terms used in verses 4 and 5 can only refer to genuine believers — 'enlightened', 'who have shared in the Holy Spirit'! And at first sight one would be inclined to agree with them. However, one term that is not used is 'believe' or 'faith', so we should pause to take a look at the surrounding verses. Note three things.

First, the whole chapter, particularly the last eight verses, is aimed at convincing the readers of their security through God's unchangeable purpose and oath. It would be strange if verses 4-6 were intended to undermine that.

Secondly, the illustration in verses 7 and 8, which is often ignored in the debate, refers simply to two kinds of people: the fruitful and the unfruitful. The fruitful are saved and the unfruitful are burned. Clearly the people described in the preceding verses are the unfruitful ones, and the rest of the New Testament tells us that such people are not real Christians (see, for example, Matthew 7:20).

Thirdly, verse 9 says that the writer is convinced of 'better things' in the case of his readers, clearly in contrast with the 'things' mentioned in verses 4-6. These 'better things' accompany salvation, so obviously the others listed in verses 5-6 do not. Whatever else is true of the characteristics described in those earlier verses, they do not necessarily accompany salvation, as do the good works done out of love for God, referred to in verse 10.

If all this surprises you, notice that in verses 4-5 there is no mention not only of faith, but also of repentance or regeneration. All the things mentioned can be true of false disciples. (Indeed, the New Testament even speaks of false disciples believing—Luke 8:13; John 8:30-31!) More accurately they could be true *then*, for it seems to me that much of what we have described here can best be understood in terms of those gifts of the Spirit which

There is no mention of faith, nor of repentance or regeneration.

were present then, but not now. 1 Corinthians 13:1-3 tells us that, far from being evidence of some higher experience of the Holy Spirit, they are not even proof of salvation! 'If I speak in the tongues of men and of angels, but have not love, I am only a resounding gong or a clanging cymbal. If I have the gift of prophecy and can fathom all mysteries and all knowledge, and if I have a faith that can move mountains, but have not love, I am nothing.'

Similarly, Matthew 7:21-23 tells us that 'disciples' can prophesy, drive out demons and perform miracles and still be excluded from the kingdom of heaven as 'evildoers'. All these things rank as sharing in the Holy Spirit, tasting the powers of the new age and being enlightened. Remember that Judas was one of the Twelve, who were given authority to cast out demons and heal miraculously (Matthew 10:1-4). Was he, in fact, such a one as these? Certainly, when he saw what he had done to our Lord, he did not repent, but only showed remorse.

Thus, as I said at the beginning of this letter, there is evidence of a working of the Holy Spirit which does not bring salvation and is not intended to do so. When we are testing a profession of faith, we must look for the evidence of a change of life. There are far too many people today whose only claim to be considered Christians is that once upon a time they made some sort of decision or engaged in some kind of Christian work.

Checking up on all this should keep

When we are testing a profession of faith, we must look for the evidence of a change of life.

you occupied for a little while. I look forward to hearing from you again after your holiday. No doubt the preachers you hear then will provide further material for enquiry.

Yours as ever — and *for* ever in Christ,

Uncle Harry

Checking up on all this should keep you occupied for a little while.

7.

The God of all grace

My dear Tom,

So now you know where I stand! Yes, I am a Calvinist or, better, I hold to Calvinistic teaching or, better still, I don't use the name at all.

John Calvin was one of the greatest of God's servants, if not the greatest, since the days of the apostles, at least as far as teaching the truth is concerned, but we are taught to call no man master, except *the* Master, and Calvin himself would certainly object to our misuse of his name. Do you know that he left instructions, when he died, that he was to be buried in an unmarked grave? When a visitor arrived in Geneva just a short while after Calvin's death, no one could show him the great Reformer's grave. His real monument is in the evangelical Protestant churches which came out of the Reformation, to which his teaching gave such stability.

Misunderstandings

Now, please don't get the idea that I'm
ashamed of the name as such. I hold the
doctrines usually called Calvinism most
strongly, as you will have gathered. It's
just the idea of man-worship that it implies to which I object. However, there are
other good reasons for avoiding the use of
the term. There are many Christians who
simply react in blind anger whenever they
hear the term, usually because they do not
understand it properly. The reason for this
varies with individuals. Some have only
met perversions of the teaching and think
that a Calvinist is someone who doesn't
preach the gospel and who doesn't believe
in evangelism or missionary work.

Others have been badly taught (or not
taught at all) and have never thought about
the subject of grace properly. They don't
realize what the real controversy is or how
it fits in with the Scriptures. Such people
may have heard of Arminianism, named
after Jacobus Arminius, and often show
their ignorance by using such statements
as, 'I'm not a Calvinist or an Arminian, but
halfway between' (or 'both at the same
time'), by which they want to say they
believe in God's grace but also in free will,
which as we've seen cannot be. Others, of
course, simply want to say they believe in
preaching the gospel, not realizing that a
stress on man's responsibility to preach,
and to believe, the gospel is part of genuine Calvinism anyway! The same failure
lies behind an assertion like, 'You must be

*Yes, I am a
Calvinist or,
better, I hold to
Calvinistic
teaching or,
better still, I
don't use the
name at all.*

a Calvinist on your knees, but an Arminian on your feet.'

The five points

A better term to use to describe the biblical
teaching about God's sovereignty in salvation is 'the doctrines of grace'. I've used
this myself quite frequently in our correspondence. These doctrines are the ones
we've been discussing over the last months
— or is it years? — and which are sometimes referred to by that somewhat strange
term you have come across — Tulip. I'm
not very keen on this at all, but it is, in fact,
a mnemonic, as follows :

> T = Total depravity
> U = Unconditional election
> L = Limited atonement
> I = Irresistible grace
> P = Perseverance

*Titles can be
misleading,
but the
'five points'
can be useful
as a frame-
work, so don't
forget them.*

You know already what I'm going to say,
don't you? These titles can be very misleading. Every time we use 'total deprav-
ity' we have to explain that it does not
mean that every individual is as bad as he
or she can be, but that sin has affected
every part of his being (the 'totality' of it).
We've already gone into the inadequacy
of 'limited' atonement and the problems
of 'irresistible' grace. However, the sum-
mary of the issues involved, known as the
five points of Calvinism, can be useful. By
the way, you almost have to learn a new

language if you want to understand some people. It is quite common in some circles, as a sort of theological shorthand, to refer simply to 'five-pointers', who believe all five doctrines, and 'four-pointers', who accept all but particular redemption.

In fact, 'the five points of Calvinism' are a misnomer anyway. It should be 'the five points of Arminianism'. It was the followers of Arminius who raised their objections to the teaching of the Reformers under five over-simplified headings, to which the orthodox party replied in these five points, at the great Synod of Dort, held in 1619. It was the 'opposition' who limited the scope of the discussion in this way, but, as I say, the 'five points' can be useful as a framework, so don't forget them.

Biblical doctrines

The real objection to the term Calvinism, of course, is that Calvin did not invent the doctrines at all. Most of what is called Calvinism, apart from being biblical, really could be referred to as Augustinianism. Augustine of Hippo, not the later man of the same name who 'ruled' in Canterbury, was a great theologian of the late fourth and early fifth centuries. I just looked up his dates (A. D. 354-430) and came across this comment, by A. M. Renwick, about his conversion: 'The spiritual change was complete. He knew it was all from the sovereign mercy of God, and henceforth, like Paul, the marvels of divine grace became his chief theme.'

> *The real objection to the term Calvinism is that Calvin did not invent the doctrines at all.*

So when Pelagius, who, by the way, was probably British, began to spread heretical teachings about free will and man's ability to save himself, Augustine was his main opponent. He reaffirmed the biblical doctrines of God's grace and succeeded in keeping the church sound on this point, at least nominally, and he had a great influence on the leading Reformers like Luther and Calvin.

Contrary to the impression you may have been given, Calvin was not a man of one doctrine, i. e. predestination. In fact, in his greatest work, *The Institutes of the Christian Religion,* Calvin did not begin with predestination as an attribute of God, as some would have expected, but placed that teaching in the context of salvation. By the way, sneers about his reference to predestination as a 'horrible decree' are quite misplaced. The original Latin simply meant, 'awesome decree', and such it certainly is. Most people are not aware that Calvin's most original contributions were on the topics of the person and work of Christ and of the Holy Spirit.

Really, you know, we are just playing with the subject. The long and short of it is that these doctrines are Pauline (i. e. from the apostle Paul, nothing to do with your cousin!), indeed biblical, from beginning to end. Both the Old and New Testaments are full of these assertions of the sovereignty of God in providence and salvation. If you read your Bible properly you simply cannot avoid this concept — and I hope that by now you wouldn't want to!

If you read your Bible properly you simply cannot avoid this concept.

Reformed doctrine

I think I have probably used the term
'Reformed' earlier to describe the doctrines
of grace. I know that it can become a rather
unhelpful catchword, almost as bad as
Calvinism, but it has its uses. In the first
place it identifies our teaching as that which
came out of the Reformation and which
the churches that originated then are
supposed to hold and proclaim (although
most of them no longer do). Thus it avoids
the unhelpful emphasis on one man.
Another virtue is this: the term 'Reformed'
stresses that we are concerned with more
than just five points about salvation. They
are central and vital, but they do not
constitute everything that 'Reformed'
teaching includes.

There is a great body of teaching that
stretches over all the doctrine of God and
man. It includes the whole work of the
Holy Spirit from inspiration to glorifi-
cation, plus the doctrine of the church. I'm
afraid there are many who hold to the five
points who have got very little further and
just do not understand the wider and
deeper elements of the Reformed faith.
There is also the idea of a 'world-view', an
attitude to the creation and the culture in
which we live, which is part of Reformed
theology, but which scarcely exists outside it. Reformed doctrine is not just one
aspect of Christian truth; it is Christianity
in its fullest and deepest form. But remember, a church is not necessarily 'Reformed'
simply because it uses the word in its title.

> *Reformed
> doctrine is not
> just one aspect
> of Christian
> truth; it is
> Christianity in
> its fullest and
> deepest form.*

More than doctrines

However, the most important thing that I want you to note is this: we are not concerned with mere doctrines about salvation, nor even with the addition of other great truths. We are concerned with God himself. Augustine, Calvin and the other Reformers, the Puritans and the great men since, were above all men of God. The Bible is not just a collection of doctrines, but a revelation of the glory, sovereignty and majesty of God. He is set before us as the one to be worshipped and praised, the one whose name is to be hallowed and magnified. This is a far greater concept than any of the individual doctrines, however much we believe and love them.

To be confronted with the Lord, as was Isaiah in the temple, or Ezekiel on the banks of the Kebar River, or Job in the storm, or Paul on the Damascus road, or John on the Isle of Patmos, is to be humbled and caused to fear and reverence, as well as love, the great and living God. It is this awe and godly fear which characterizes the Reformed Christian, which governs both his worship, his life and his evangelism. Without this, belief of the doctrines is a cold and lifeless intellectualism, in which man is exalted instead of being humbled. That must be avoided at all costs. The real spirit of the Reformed faith — true Calvinism if you wish — is to be found in the words of the great apostle in Romans 11:33-36:

> 'Oh, the depth of the riches of the
> wisdom and knowledge of God!

We are not concerned with mere doctrines but with God himself.

How unsearchable his judgements,
and his paths beyond tracing out!
"Who has known the mind of the Lord?
Or who has been his counsellor?"
"Who has ever given to God,
that God should repay him?"
For from him and through him and to
him are all things.
To him be the glory for ever! Amen.'

After that, what is there left to say? I commit
you to God and his grace — that grace
which 'was given us in Christ Jesus before
the beginning of time' (2 Timothy 1:9), and
in which we are called to be strong (2
Timothy 2:1). If you accept and practise
what I've been trying to get over to you, it
won't make you popular, but God will be
with you.

I look forward to hearing from you, or
perhaps even seeing you.

Yours by sovereign grace,

Uncle Harry

> *If you accept and practise what I've been trying to get over to you, it won't make you popular, but God will be with you.*

Postscript

Postscript

Dear Tom,

It occurs to me that, although I've quoted Scripture frequently in my letters, you might appreciate a few more references to look up — just in case you still have any lingering doubts as to whether this teaching is biblical. I will arrange them under the five basic doctrines.

1. Total inability

Genesis 6:5; 8:21; Psalm 51:5; Jeremiah 17:9; Mark 7:20-23; John 8:34; Romans 8:5-8; 1 Corinthians 2:14; 2 Corinthians 4:3-4.

2. Unconditional election

Deuteronomy 7:6-8; John 10:16; 17:2; Acts 13:48; 18:9-10; Romans 9:11, 22-24; 1 Corinthians 1:26-29; Ephesians 1:4-5; Colossians 3:12.

3. Particular redemption

Exodus 12:3-4; Isaiah 53:8; Matthew 1:21; John 10:11, 15; 15:13; 17:9; Acts 20:28; Ephesians 5:25-27; 1 Peter 1:18-19.

4. Unconquerable grace

Ezekiel 36:26; John 3:3-8; 6:37, 44-45, 65; Acts 11:18; 2 Corinthians 5:17; Ephesians 2:8-9; Philippians 1:29; 2 Thessalonians 2:13-14; Hebrews 12:2; 1 Peter 2:9.

5. Final perseverance

Luke 22:32; John 10:28-29; Romans 5:8-10; 8:28-30; Philippians 1:6; 2 Timothy 1:12; 4:18; Hebrews 6:17-19; 7:25; 1 John 5:18.

Only a short letter, but there were too many references to fit on a postcard!

Looking forward to seeing you,

Yours by God's grace,

Uncle Harry

... just in case you still have any lingering doubts as to whether this teaching is biblical.